Poetically in Motion

Toriana Williams

Poetically in Motion

by

Toriana Williams

ISBN: 979-8-9858131-3-5

Library of Congress Control Number: 2022905926

Cover design: Sadia Zulfiqar

Published by G Publishing, LLC

Edited by Anthony Ambrogio

Printed in the United States of America.

Special Thanks

To publisher Julia Hunter for her help in preparing this manuscript and seeing it through to publication.

To "Poetry in the Boro," my very first open-mic experience and the first poetry community that made me feel welcome.

To "Under 1 Roof," for allowing me the opportunity to be the very first artist to grace their stage and who provided my first paid performance.

Shout out to Laura Bester Brown for giving me the tools to self publish and the confidence that I could be an author.

Shout out to Kory Wells, Poet Laureate of Murfreesboro, TN who has inspired me to write a few pieces in my book today with her word challenges.

And lastly, many thanks to my mother, Catina Williams, who has always believed in me, even when I was too insecure and afraid to believe in myself.

Thank you all so very much.

An Ode to Procrastination

Stagnation is the enemy of growth
Stationary existing
Waiting to be summoned
By someone
other than charging head first
Unto a new chapter
Fear has captured my attention
Missing windows of opportunities
Have suddenly changed my view
Made me uncomfortable in this position
I'm now on a mission to
Go after what I want
Create the life that I want
Feel the pain and the excitement
And continue to use
Literature as my escape from
Reality.
No more stalling
No more excuses
No more doing things last minute
I will begin a new literary movement
Conversational poetry

I'm talking to you but
I'm talking to myself first
I hope you enjoy what you read
I know I loved writing everything you see

Table of Contents

Follow Me If You Can

Marching to the beat of my own drum
You can't match my pace
Each step is a place in time
Do not ask me
What's on my mind.
My smile
Is my weapon of *design*
to trick those into thinking
I'm blind to the madness.
The saddest thing
is when they underestimate me.
Stride by stride
My psyche reminds me
To be
Proud of who I am.
Unwavering
Steadfast in my beliefs.
I am not playing follow the leader
I'm landscaping my own reality.
While marching to the beat of my own drum
You can walk with me
If—
You can catch the rhythm...

Toriana Williams

The Times

Viewing life through different lenses
Enemies are treated as friends
Where are our Heroes?
The meek are getting **bold**
Blatant racism exposed.
Truth being faded out by lies
Tears fall while mothers cry
No one minds.
Who can I trust?
I see that look in your eyes.
Why
can't I
trust you?
We should be standing side by side.
Skinfolk ain't always Kin-folk
I learned that through time.
Some want to be viewed as equals
I want *everyone* to shine.
Being self aware and intelligent seems like a crime
I think I may be wasting my own time...
No one wants to
really make a change
They just like to complain online.

Angered Soul

Angry soul

One day

That bad attitude has got to go.

Depression is one thing

Anguish

is another.

Do you think that anger helps you uncover the truth?

Wasting your youth on nonsense.

Being hostile

instead of modest.

Trying your hardest to prove your strength

You fail to realize

there is power in *silence* and humility.

Disrupted soul

your world will never be filled with tranquility.

If you continue to

react to life through

Anger!

Instead of civility.

Toriana Williams

Conflicted

Pondering everything
My face
My shape
My place in society
Good is never
Good enough
Happiness must come with lots of bucks
Am I nothing without currency?
Beauty is now prescribed and
Validated online
What a time to be alive!
Smoking heavy so I don't lose my mind
Sedatives added
to slow   down   time
Politics?
A circus that many don't want to attend
Let's pretend that
our lives are not insignificant.
Watch the News
use **pigment** as a muse for misjudgment

Log on to social media,
read the comments.
Oddest thing is
Why do I even care?
Demanding respect for other people
is not my cross to bear.
Should I just live blissfully amidst despair?

Toriana Williams

Notebook

Since learning the ability to write
I knew I had a place where
my inner thoughts didn't have to hide.
In my notebook,
Journal or diary
I have a blank space that is always welcoming
On those pages I can be *free*,
On those pages I have someone there
willing to listen to me,
who doesn't judge
and above all
I can release my emotions without
Anyone watching me.
Why can't everyone be like a notebook?
Inviting and willing to adapt to
Any emotion
Any idea
Theory or poem.
Even as a writer I am not like a notebook
I have my own thoughts and perceptions
I admit

I have judged others before looking at my reflection,

Everyone has their imperfections.

That's why a notebook is what I strive to be

I want to always be open to new possibilities.

Toriana Williams

Ad Nauseam

Cops have him in a tight squeeze.
The suspect's thinking
Is anyone going to emancipate me?
Twenty bystanders holding camera phones and
the cops get off scot-free.
America you haven't changed much I see.
Back in the day
When it was legal
To have my ancestors working three shifts without pay.
The consequence of asking for mercy
was even more pain
No way.
Today,
I sit and watch the news
Drinking wine trying not to get the blues.
Keeping my happiness on reserve
For when I hear some good news.
I know this subject can get annoying to
all those who have the
Superpower of privilege protecting you.

When the boys in blue

see people with **noir** skin

they shoot to kill

Not to subdue.

I am tired of

Talking about this subject too.

How many more people have to *die* until everyone gets tired too?

Toriana Williams

Loser's Game

I don't want to be famous
I want to be the person who epitomizes success.
While you try your best
To make ends meet
And retreat
To your nice apartment,
I want to be the owner
who rakes in all of your profit and
While you fight over materialistic things,
I will be *traveling*.
When you have to pinch and save your coins for a six-bedroom house,
Me and my spouse
Will be eating *foie gras* in our fabulous mansion,
Ducked off by an ocean
Isolated
so no one
will actually
see my hatred
As I collect all of your checks
And you still believe

the small things in life are the best.
See, I don’t want to just be rich,
I want to be the person calling the shots
Even having a shot as president.
I don’t want to be a participant in the game
I want to be a graphic designer
Making it.

Toriana Williams

Playtime Is Over

Equality

A lie they fed us

So that we are subconsciously

living in the American dream.

Illusion of understanding

Pandering to the hope inside of the virtually hopeless… but

Racism is still in existence

Documenting charity as good will

they are playing in our faces

Make it make sense

we turn everything into a trend

Pain into music

Distress into poetry

Struggle into fashion

Scraps into a feast.

We are Adaptable beyond belief

Picture this

If I bend down and do some crazy spin move

And add a little groove to it

I will go viral

gather some nice views
but if someone **copies** it and
Extracts flavor from it
they will get endorsements
and become famous.
You all are aware of this
It's a sad truth
I am not your equal
you cannot fathom the strength it takes to be me
You do not bring positivity ultimately
Constantly studying me trying to be like me but
A carbon copy can never compare to the real thing.
You don't see
they're playing in our faces
Laughing at us
Will arrest you for hurting an animal
Petition if a dog is mistreated
Yet turn around and make support pages
For murder suspects
Not the victims,
I thought all lives mattered but
Hey, they must've done something to deserve it…

is what they usually say.

System is rigged

Justice?

doesn't exist in our government

Ill intent written in every amendment

and the laws

A quick Pause

I would like to say

This is my therapy writing my feelings because If I don't

no one will speak them for me unfortunately

This world isn't simply black & white

It's us melanated ones

who want true freedom

against everyone...

If you believe we are really alpha and omega

That means we can change this world expeditiously & easily

Tired of witnessing people

playing in my face

I'm ready to

End this game

Man in the Mirror

The emptiest minds think the loudest
Are the proudest and
have enough confidence
to get the attention that I,
I mean we shy people deserve.
We have the brightest ideas but
the smallest voices.
Strongest concepts but are afraid
to unravel the truth.
I blame people like me
Who hoard their wisdom internally.
We gave those who have ill will the platform
to spew hate,
lies and/or
Advocate things that shouldn't be okay.
We sit on our couches and judge those in celebrity roles but
Are too afraid to audition.
Sadly the next generation are the victims.
I sit in my mind battling anxiety
when I could be informing,

brainstorming ways to help society.

The youth are being misguided and

my silly fear is no excuse to watch them burn and

Not learn valuable information.

I'm exhibiting selfish behavior,

My thought process may not be popular but it's needed.

Thinking on your own and

Not following trends

When will this way of thinking begin, again?

Never, if we continue to let our personal fears win.

A Constant Reminder

Blind in our current situation
Amendments still need adjustments
Duped into believing they would play fair
No matter where I go they're always there.
Infatuated with power
bending the rules
is a common practice certain people choose.
Colonialism,
religious take-overs,
building walls
declaring war
creating borders,
New world order.
Changing history, hiding the truth
They should really be
afraid of fate for their sake
Knowing these things fills many with rage,
I want to leave but it's not going away.
The stories of those once in chains
Marching for freedom,
Carving their own lane in time

Toriana Williams

Never leave my mind.
How can one forget that blacks were once property?
Stripped of their rights and
living in conditions worse than poverty.
Danced and pranced for some respect
Tried to be "good"
so they didn't see an untimely death.
Prayed for better days,
asked God for guidance
He sent Moses to lead the way.
The past isn't a burden but
A reminder
to never let it repeat again.

Fight

Backed into a corner
Must try to survive
Once had an army
A team, family
Now this wall is the only place
for you to hide.
Swallow your pride
Do you fight or fly?
Take over the room
One-man artillery
Who can destroy whatever approaches
That'll be a battle of course but
whose side are you on?
I hope your own

Toriana Williams

Pretty

What does it mean to be pretty?
Should I wear my hair curly and
Act narcissistically?
Do I need makeup
to build a foundation for myself?
I need materialistic things
to feel complete?
So I have to wear a mask
in order to ask people to respect me?
My eyebrows have to be on *fleek*
In order for you to speak to me?
How wonderful this world would be
if your character was judged
not your beauty.
Which I thought was only skin deep yet
if I don't make your peter peak
You will not seek my attention.
Did I forget to mention
That there're women out there
whose curves dance in the wind *naturally,*

NO silicone or plastic covering.
Have full lips no collagen
Real flesh without powdery substances
Hair blooming from the scalp
no matter the *texture* or length.
I repeat,
what does it mean to be pretty?
Wait so I can't chill with the fellas and act silly?
I have to wear a frilly dress
that shows off my chest
Is that really the best way to live life?
Well I have no interest in being pretty.
If it means that
I have to wear a mask and
I can't be silly.
I really wish those
who wake up themselves and
boldly go out into the real world
Fresh faced and free
Were praised.
Instead of being called
Lame, basic, or gay.

Toriana Williams

Wouldn’t that be the day?
Be who you are regardless,
I know this may be the hardest concept to grasp,
That mask of clay will never stay
Even if you put it on every day.
Your real face still exists and
When you meet your **prince**
and he wants to **kiss** your cheek, makeup free
When you take your makeup off
Aren’t you still pretty?

Tunnel Vision

I know you see me because
I see you
The hate in your heart is easy for you to cover if
I'm in a position that's subservient to you
Piercing eyes of blue
came from the Motherland too.
Recessive genes
Made them royalty
so they believe.
Achieved their dream of colonizing
because they cannot simply create
Like we holders of
Dominant genes.
Found the means to damaging
The minds of melanated beings
who run afraid of injustice
That we wouldn't face
If we
Rise like Maya and
Sting like Ali.
I'll quietly

continue to view racism
For what it is
evil ingenuity.

Baggage Claim

Bag lady
carrying a precious cargo
Once had a heart of gold but
It has eroded.
Scolded by loves past.
lugging her load
Not knowing the next road.
Poor Packages
shipped against their will.
Meeting people
unworthy of their presence.
It makes no sense
Being held hostage in life
They didn't ask to be here.
Mistreated and ridiculed
as if they're the ones who
dumped their sac of false hope into you.
Suitcase ripped to bits
Been cascading on tough terrain.
Explain

Toriana Williams

How is everyone's life so special again?
Carrying on
Without a clue
As to why
Shipping and handling was free but
The destination was devastating.
Cells and particles
made to form lots of sad lives.
Eyes crying more than smiling
Thinking about just dying.
Trying to find the answer to life.
Realizing you're just existing
Tell how wonderful it is having and
how much you
Love your *accessory*.
Unless you're toting a sweet bag and
have help with unloading responsibility
Do not nag others about
being baggage free.
Sadly
Some purses feel cursed
and rather be in a hearse than on earth.

Others are designer
living finer than most and
can boast about their travels.
Everyone's journey is different
how others' luggage arrived and
survived is not always pretty.
Keep that in mind.

Toriana Williams

Emotional Fitness

When the heart works for itself
to keep the body well and
Doesn't dwell on sentimental things
The results can be amazing.
Gazing into the eyes of someone
Who is ultimately a waste of time can get tiring.
Wheezing for air
When you could repair your surroundings.
Sounding like
Solidarity inhibits prosperity
Or
Being alone doesn't mean you're lonely.
You're only conspiring a plan
to gather all the love you can and
Giving it to yourself first.
Thirsting for affection
Instead of personal reflection
Never ends well.
Think about the things you could be doing
that don't involve losing yourself.
Do not compromise your health
build emotional wealth within and
Begin a new life.

Distorted Vision

When you see a young black man drowning
Do you try to save him?
Is it wrong for him to try to save himself because
he knows no one will come help?
When he has to pick himself up by his bootstraps,
Is it wrong that he does some unconventional things
to make sure that he eats?
If you're not going to feed me
I'm going to eat regardless
Is that a wrong mindset to have?
So when he joins the only family
He thinks he has
To make sure they all eat.
Why are people so oblivious of the pain
he had to endure before
Being involved in the streets?
As if his life was peaches and cream and
that his family had a piece of the American Dream
Well that's false
When you don't have any positive role models
who are you most likely to follow?
When you have to feed yourself
regardless if you play the lotto.

Toriana Williams

When your motto goes from shoot for the stars
To I'll get mine by any means,
Do you always think he is living
his life contrary
to his upbringing?
It's a dog-eat-dog world and
being prepared for battle is his upbringing.
In no way am I encouraging engaging in criminal activity but
One must remember
There's always a starting point.
So when you see them smoking their cigarettes and
Lighting their joints there's an inner sadness
Hidden behind the mask.
I see you trying to be the best man you know how to be and
If it's a crime
Then help him.
When you see a young black man drowning
Do you walk by and give him the evil eye
for trying to save himself
Or do you help?
I see you, young man; my vision isn't distorted.

The Media Doesn't Speak for Me

The media dehumanized us
By calling us *Super-predators*
A Terror to the streets
To criminalize us.
So while the world sees us down
The government can kick us off our feet.
Which makes everyone skip past the real enemy:
That little box
Filled with lies and propaganda
Planted in our faces.
So when the man gets ahold of me
There will be no mercy
He sees me as a threat and nothing else
A pest to be eradicated.
Can't wait for the moment to police us
Just to Mistreat us.
But let the media tell it
We're just making this all up.
Why is it that when you see someone wearing a hoodie
You're scared suddenly?

Toriana Williams

Do you think that's coincidental?
No
it's from your TV.
Criminals, thugs, ruthless killers
Seeing black people paraded on TV
Marching into prison.
This image was implanted.
Since the birth of a nation,
This nation and the media
have manipulated the minds of the masses
All I ask is
How many black people have you personally met
Who were hell bent on causing white fury?
Versus the number of black people trying
Their best to survive and thrive like everyone else?
A *Wise* man once said,
The media has the power to make the guilty look innocent and
The innocent look guilty.
We have the power to look at people individually.
So simply
Look at me with your lenses bias-free and
Watch how differently you'll see me

Versus what you see on TV.
Remember
The media does not speak for me.

Toriana Williams

Warriors Way

Can you hear the beating heart of the warrior?
Resurrected by destruction and rage.
The echoing has been calling our names.
It's a shame
Not many hear the pulsing in their ears
As they continue to rally around their distracted peers.
If many really believed so heavily in
Dr. Martin Luther King Jr's dream
It wouldn't have been replaced with self hate.
You can repeat his speech but
If your heart is weak
You will never reach the promised land.
I'm not talking about after death
I want my flowers now
While I'm alive.
I preach unity—they laugh at me,
If I complain and exclaim the names of
victims of racism
I'm suddenly awake.
Send my condolences but

Does that really alleviate the victim's family pain?
We need to change some things
There are so many deceased
to only mention the ones who were slain recently
Is a travesty and
it's really sad to see
History continuously repeating itself.
We know the problems
Do you know your enemy?
I don't think so
You're too forgiving
Smile in their faces
Yet mean-mug me.
Or maybe I can only hear the heartbeat
I'll find those
Who hear it with me

Toriana Williams

Chameleon

You call yourself adaptable
Unfortunately you are expendable.
Depending upon your mood
Your demeanor is interchangeable.
You think you're slick
Changing your colors depending on a person's skin.
You make me sick in the worst way.
They say flattery will get you anywhere.
Wherever you go
Just know
You come from somewhere **dark** and inescapable.
They say cooning,
You say survival,
They say….
You say….
I say deplorable.
Even if you're able to achieve things
By adding heavy cream to your coffee
Remember that the bean is dark on the tree.
So without darkness

You wouldn't have anything to lighten, sadly.
Wake up lizard
Your true colors have always been seen,
No need to keep hiding.

Toriana Williams

Manipulation

I was engulfed in you.
So saturated that
I couldn't see myself
While
I was with you
Me and you were
Connected.
Like an adhesive
You had me stuck
I was attached
Thought I was in luck
That glue was abrasive.
You were very persuasive.
You had me convinced that
Without you
My life will be filled with
Loneliness.
That when you touched me
You were the best to ever
Caress me
That your persistent presence meant

You were in love with me, but
You manipulated me.
Took my mind and
Molded it to your liking.
When I look in the mirror
I don't recognize the eyes
Staring back at me.
That smile you see is
Crying inside.
Now all I want to do is hide
From the world
You told me that I was your world,
What is a girl to do?
Why am I asking you this?
I know what to do.
Get glue remover
So I can get unstuck
Live my life
Get away
Cut the strings
I am not your puppet,
Take my life back!

Toriana Williams

I don't care
About all of the good things
in the past.
I allowed you to
Control me too long
Those feelings in my heart
have long passed.
I am free now
I will never return to captivity.
Manipulate whoever you want.
I know
It won't be me.

Sleepless Nights

Why does it seem like
the ones that do wrong
Never lose sleep?
While I weep at 3 a.m.
about my hurt feelings
You're just chilling.
As I toss and turn
You don't learn from your mistakes.
What's great is
While I lose an everlasting battle with my mind
Trying to make sense of this mess
You couldn't care less
About my inability to find happiness
Enough to fall asleep.
It would be sweet if
I could beat up my brain
To just stop it from rewinding the pain you caused.
I tried to press pause
My heart and mind need recalibration
As thoughts go through my mind about retaliation
You have no clue what the situation

has done to me while you sleep
ever so peacefully.
You would think those who do wrong
Couldn't sleep at night
That's not quite right
See only you and me understand
the damage and cannot manage to keep it together.
When I try to sleep my mind repeats
the things you've done to me.
Possibly you just don't care and
I bear all of your feelings upon me
While I lose sleep.

Being Black

What happened to being black?
When we didn't allow our people to get off track towards success?
When you always wished another brother or sister the best.
What happened to being black?
Even when the world turned their backs on us,
we had our own.
When calling out for unity was as easy as throwing a block party.
What happened to being black?
When you loved your skin and
regardless of how the TV portrayed us,
We knew our inner king and queen.
So those images on the screen
Would not chip away at our self esteem.
What happened to being black?
When respect was the major focus.
When we raised our kids
so forget what the TV says,
"I can't discipline my child?

Well take 'em you'll bring them right back."
What happened to being black?
Where cultural appropriation
was an action on a regular basis
Yet it never fazed us,
Because
We knew we were the best
& they wanted to be us.
What happened to being black?
When we didn't let whack rappers tell us to disrespect our women,
Put drugs in our systems and
Advocate going to prison.
What happened to being black?
When you'll be disgraced for being ignorant,
Not praised and given millions to poison the youth.
I'm sorry but that's the truth
We lost love for ourselves
That's when our race started going to hell.
What happened to being black?
When our young brothers didn't feel they needed to be strapped,

because their minds were not wrapped around gangs.
When your left fist and right fist
Finished the beef that day.
What happened to being black?
When your favorite celebrity
Did Not avoid speaking of being a minority, and
the majority of their career inspired you
To become the best black person you could be.
What happened to being black?
I'm not sure I'm at a loss
Remember when being black was awesome and
We actually loved one another?
If another soul spoke badly about our bronzed skin and
our hair with kinks
We knew it was jealousy
So we turned the other cheek.
I love being black
I'm just waiting on more black people
To come on board with me.

Misery Loves Company

Misguided individuals hungering for misunderstanding
Misleading others into
involving themselves with their misfortune.
Brought about not by mistakes but
by intentionally damaging the ill-informed.
Persuading others to join their hazardous paths of pain.
Mishaps not mentioned because of hidden missions
Agendas even.
Misery isn't always detectable
It is sometimes burrowing lurking
looking for a naïve host.
Who is easily subjugated to their inevitable malevolent presence.
Beware of who you allow close to you
Your positive energy can be magnetic
There's no coincidence that their wickedness found you.

Tolerance

Why do you hate me?
Well if that's not the case,
Why wouldn't you date me?
Complain about me being here
it's clear you don't like me,
Why?
I'm trying to take things at face value.
My presence is not your preference I guess
So you must feel unvalued
Sad realizing times are changing
Is it hard to let people go about their way?
Allowing them freedom to be themselves in every way?
Your pride can't reside in the back of your mind
Where everyone's bad thoughts hide.
Do you need to show your dominance at all times?
Will standing next to me make you feel weak?
Would your tongue fall out your mouth
if we were to speak?
Does my Aura reek of self-confidence?
Or are you frightened that one day

We'll tread on your land and

Give you the same treatment if ever given the upper hand?

What if I told you that wasn't the plan?

Yes, every dog has his day but

that gift of retribution isn't only given to few.

It's received by all those who are willing to co-exist without prejudice.

Who, What, When, Where, and Why?

Who did this to us?
Made of us some evil.
Born of pure heart but somehow misled.
Who fed you lies and made your vibrant heart dull?
Who erupted the darkness inside of you?
What evil thing burrowed in your psyche
that makes you think you're better than me?
What past lessons have you misinterpreted?
What media propaganda sites have infiltrated your head?
When will real change come?
When are we going to learn we all come from the same home?
Where can I go where love outweighs hate?
Where is heaven?
I wanna see the pearly gates.
Where can I stand in line?
Should I just follow the songs of those slain
from pain inflicted in the past and today?
Why do we have to keep trying to get along?

Toriana Williams

Why isn’t tolerance more natural than politics?

Why haven’t you woken up?

Why do we keep trying to educate, entertain, and be included?

Yes… I've Been Abused

I lied to myself
Made myself believe that
if I kept my enemy close that somehow he wouldn't harm me.
I fooled myself to believe that
if he hits me and says sorry he means it.
That since I'm now single,
I'm also free from this
Self-loathing demon
but I miscalculated.
Just because he cannot slap me again
That doesn't mean
My self-inflicted abuse will also end.
I have to begin loving myself unconditionally
That is no longer an option.
They say sticks and stones will break my bones
but words will never hurt me, but
Why do I still find myself crying
after the insults you hurled at me?
Why are you still on my mind?
I should hate you but I was so blinded by love

If I hate you now I hated myself back then too.

I fell for this trick time and time again…

He'd get on his knees and beg me for one more chance again,

Even cry and shout out to God asking *why must we end*?!

And wanna talk about marriage and

Tell me about plans for our future that he made in his head.

I scoff and ignore him for a week or two but somehow

he'll slither back in my life—**snake**

Who convinced Eve to ruin Eden

Some men out here

feel as if they have control over you,

that since you gave them a sample of your heart and

other parts of your body they deserve you.

Girls, do not listen to those fools.

When I saw myself *abused* on wet streets in the middle of the night

I knew then

that this love I thought I was in wasn't right for me and

that I've lied to myself one too many times.

I'd be damned if I let the enemy kill me and
I have to watch my family bury me on A&E
from a tv in the clouds,
because he said that if he abused me he loved me
Uncontrollably.
Well, now
I love myself even more
He may not have taught me much but
He did teach me that
no man can break me.

Toriana Williams

A Haunting Within

Rain drops tumbling down my gutter
Tears stream softly down my face, but
I do not utter a sound.
Why cry when everyone is asleep?
So I can let out the pain and
hopefully the man upstairs hears me.
Please stop these thoughts from lingering.
Repeating images of the things
that never seem to haunt me when the sun is beaming.
Only when I'm dreaming,
Do these sad and nasty things reappear
I don't want this on my conscience
I'm trying my hardest to be in control.
Brain, you stay out of that dark hole you call the past.
Tired of depression anxiously waiting to attack
Breathing every breathe
As if it were my last.
Trying to grasp onto reality, but
The past can make seeing the present cloudy.

Thought if I pretended it never happened
It will all go away.
PTSD is a serious thing if not addressed
Or corrected
Overcompensated love to mask the pain.
Emotional war internally will drive anyone insane
Most people don't understand and
it's just too hard to explain.

Toriana Williams

With or Within

Do you want to be with me or within me?

Do you like me as a human being?

My flesh, my mind, my soul

Or do you just want to enter into my realm and go

On to the next girl,

Feeding her all the fluff she wants to hear?

Entangled into your promises

Attached to your every word.

Is this the type of treatment every girl receives in your world?

So when I ask "Do you want to be with me or within me?" I mean this.

After that first kiss

That first bit of contact.

What if we were unknowingly forced to sign a contract

stating that we truly want to give this a chance?

Would you sign it?

Or were you only interested in laying in it?

What's your ultimate goal?

If it's just to fill a few of my holes I'll pass.

Am I being too crass by asking straightforward "Do you want to be with me or within me?"

Don't you dare say both because

You know what I mean.

My ultimate goal is that I want everything happiness can bring.

When push comes to shove and

we have to announce our vows in front of the man above,

When we have to proudly proclaim our love

in a room full of our peers.

Would you say I do?

Or would you disappear?

Do you want to be with me or within me?

Trauma Doesn’t Exist

The past was yesterday
You can never repeat the day
Decisions were made
The time will never be refunded
No back pay.
Every day it is our responsibility to
Secure our future
Trauma only follows those who will not let go
Terrified that you’ll forget and
be in the same predicament.
Fear attached like a succubus but you must
Remove the parasite.
I mean you because no one will ever do it for you.
After it has gotten comfortable
you’ve psychologically allowed that parasite to become part you.
Inner consciousness taking away your own confidence
Beating yourself up before picking the gloves up to fight.
Do not become one with the parasite

Feed it affirmations,

logically diffuse a situation

Do not let emotion be the causation of your
personal depression.

Education of self and reflection is key,

I'm still a work in progress

Telling myself the past doesn't stop or define me

Toriana Williams

Sobriety Is Calling My Name

Saw an image of myself that I didn't recognize.

All I saw was bad circumstances and sadness in my eyes.

I need to uproot my life,

Press pause and rewind

to a happier time in my mind.

Brain clouded by smoke and mental illnesses,

Heavy medicating just to deal with today, well every day.

Addicted to the feeling of I don't care about anything

when in actuality

I care about everything.

Drinking and geeking have done nothing but

keep me going at a medium pace.

I wanna be able to face my problems sober,

not just for the moment but forever.

Not just today,

while my mind screams for weed and a drink to relax me.

I want to be in my own ear saying

"You don't have to lean on substances.

You control your life and
no matter how many hits or shots you take
it cannot make the trying times of your life go away.
You can only truly escape with a mind that's clear
It helps to shift gears towards your new existence.
Be persistent in regathering yourself, & it's okay to ask for help if needed."
The journey to sobriety is a long one and I will be triumphant in my battle.
A change of scenery and emotional support is always needed.
P.S. Your consumption is your business
I am no one to judge; just try not to over indulge and
Escape reality like I did.
I am disgusted that my name became synonymous with being
Under the influence of something.
This is why I am detoxifying my life.
Wish me luck & do not judge me on my path to clean living.

Toriana Williams

Release the Shackles

The powers-that-be
Want everyone to be blinded sheep
So we can't see the person next to us weep
about the misfortunes they've endured.
They want to make sure some get all the praise.
They never mention the days when
the poor get poorer and the beggar passes away.
Kill those who want to help
then bash us for not helping ourselves.
Are you really dividing a nation,
killing children and
turning a blind eye to poverty to accumulate personal wealth?
Is the money worth it if you have to extract all of the Earth's resources
And a once-vibrant terrain becomes a lifeless shame?
Does anyone care about the pain felt every day?
If so,
Why, when there's a chance for liberation,
is it ended in the most heinous way?
Which strikes fear that things will never get better.
Well I'm here to tell you not to look for them to change the weather.

You can ride the storm until the sun peeks out and
Shout "A new day is rising!"
Then we'll be surprising those
who thought our demise was close and
They'll realize we are wise enough
To control our own lives and say enough is enough.
Let us be tough and fight this colossal demon
so in victory we can say we won.
There needs to be unity
meaning you and me
regardless of ethnicity
as you can see
Evil destroying what makes us all happy.
No more sappy sayings,
No more asking for compassion;
let us thrash them where they stand
So we can begin a new life
Without a painful knife in our backs
making us lose track of our actual enemy.
Stand with me as we prepare for battles that will
release
All of our shackles.

Toriana Williams

Storytellers

Everyone has a story that hasn't been told
There's always truth to unfold.
Closets to be opened, doors to be shut
skeletons in the yard to be dug up but
There's a hidden gem inside of all of us
That just can't give up on the concept of success.
The inner you that knows what's best.
Your personal narrator
Scribing every page of your best-selling novel.
Remember just because there are climactic scenes,
dramatic pauses, and maybe
A huge plot twist or theatrical breakdown
Do not let the complexities inside your book
Leave the cover faced down,
shredded and torn to pieces.
Do not let the subjects inside your book
make anyone afraid to check out the thesis
Live life and continue to add writing to your pages
Keep growing and learning through all stages.
When you flip through your pages for a final read
You can look at the cover and say

I did an amazing job Indeed.

Keeping my personal knowledge on those pages
and

not letting life graze my cover.

Everyone wants to read a book in good to mint
condition

not tattered and destroyed. Why? Because

You don't want to distract them from the premise.

Toriana Williams

Cold Hard Truth

The most unprotected women in America
We know this
We are the most educated
Graduating in higher numbers than the masses
Yet reduced to the size of our asses
Classy women barely exist them girls lame they
    can't hang
Vixens riding in new whips making big chips
Yet still don't get respect for shit
Women impregnated and left like bitches I mean
    dogs
All because we let you enter without probable cause
Applause for those queens
who haven't given up on Kings because
A lot of these sheep I mean men
have been leading us astray.
Even see our struggles and
will still subject us to pain.
Products of single mothers and
Still believing we are unworthy of a ring
Chivalry has been dead what more can I explain

Thinking they're the prize
when we created the game
What a shame.
Kings aren't even laying their jackets on puddles for us
Do you really think they'll stand on the front lines and protect us?
If you're offended when reading this
Prove me wrong with action
Words mean nothing ultimately and
I refuse to sacrifice my time trying to educate you!
We can dance and party all night long
We also need to learn to shoot
Buying bundles means we can afford guns too.
Queens save your own souls because
No one is coming to save you.
I had to come remind you

Toriana Williams

America the Beautiful (Melting Pot)

How can one make America Great
without the help of other races?
This place has become this beautiful thriving country
due to the hard work and sacrifices of minorities.
Every vegetable eaten,
every cotton fiber worn,
every railroad track ridden,
every building in NYC inhabited
has been picked, sewn, laid, and built by the hands of people who look like me and
whatever new color of torment
Did you forget?
When colonizers were shipped to this seemingly vacant place.
They were sent on a mission to create another land
to be at the command of England.
So they fought for their freedom,
Did you forget that we helped you win?
That, when all men were created equal,
My ancestors were locked down and not treated as people? But

today I can stand and say my piece without getting hung from a tree because

Now it's okay that I can read.

You'd think America has gotten better than the place it used to be.

We the people made this land free

We the people fight in wars and keep families safe from harm and

we've been doing this since my ancestors were brought here as slaves, like

Every minority race, who are American citizens but

are frequently told to go back "home."

What if we left or never came,

how would America be?

So just like you're entitled to this country

so are we.

We have all bled blood on these streets and

without us America wouldn't be the wonderful land that you see.

America you are beautiful and

you wouldn't be without minorities.

Toriana Williams

Send Me Back in Time

I begged to grow up,
I yearned to have control of my life.
Went against those who tried to teach me right.
To ultimately think that
Adulting really isn't the best life.
I traded Barbie dolls for responsibility
I remember when an ice-cream cone with sprinkles was all I needed to heal.
When everything that I stressed about
wasn't really a big deal.
Now I have bills that won't go away.
I really miss when not getting what I wanted on my Christmas list was the biggest diss.
Now I have tense conversations about
why you're no longer interested and
Would like to end this.
They tried to warn me
High school will be gone before you know it
Being grown isn't all that it's cracked to be.
I would rather go to those terrible school dances,
where chances of getting drugged

are far less than in a nightclub.

I remember when staying up late doing homework
was midnight.

Now I have to calculate the amount of hours

I have until daylight to finish my homework

right after I clock out of work.

I remember when deciding if I have enough time to
eat or sleep

wasn't a thought I've came across.

Now I hate my boss 'way more than homeroom.

Arguing about music was better than arguing about
politics.

Man I wish I didn't grow into adulthood.

This life really isn't that good.

When they asked what do you want to be when you
grow up,

I should've said,

a kid again if I could.

Toriana Williams

Alive Forever

To be received by the masses?
Does that mean I compromised something or
Most likely obtained tons of fans and
or haters waiting on me to fail
Keeping a large circle without fame is a pain.
Real relationships are hard to maintain
Celebrities or the successful
say more money more problems
every gender
every generation
As if being distressed is sensational
I don't wanna be famous
I want my words to live on
I want to know I helped my people no matter how minimal
Instead of watching us behave so trivial
Instead of Sharing inspirational memes
Gotta watch what I post on social media
to avoid cancellation
trying to hide my pride subliminally
Seething, wanting

to have the freedom of people
living blissfully unaware
How dare I read and
Need to understand complex things
Like why everything we do
The world hates yet copies?
Don't stop me now
I've realized I'm Queen,
like Freddie Mercury.

Toriana Williams

Quarantine 2020

Living history
Where will you be when this is all over?
When will this ever end?
Being quarantined currently but
a month ago I guess our country just didn't see this coming?
Or the local news didn't push this particular agenda
Come to think of it most things in history are never recorded accurately.
The truth is usually buried in the bodies of the deceased.
What happens if we all live through this disease?
Are we gonna keep fighting against things that would make us a more even society?
If not why not just start attacking our enemies?
Oh yeah we're being self quarantined
War solves nothing
So you all finally see that this country's favorite color is not white it is green
Without currency your needs mean nothing.
Reality has smacked America in the face and
we have the choice to either learn or
Crash and burn…

My Poetry

I don't need a soundtrack
so you can hear the whip hit the slaves back
you know the sound.
Props and special made costumes to fuel artwork is cool.
My muse is just words
Written so eloquently that
comprehension is needed to connect to my writing spiritually
I'm not nice enough to tone it down because
If you're unaware stay that way.
No need to enlighten those whose lights have been dimmed by society
Or themselves
willingly.
If you are looking for the regurgitated flow of "woke" poetry,
You will not find it with me.
My flow matches my rhyme schemes
so every piece I write,
I recite differently.
I know I'm not in a lane,

Toriana Williams

I like to carve my own path.

My bad if you're not prepared for what I have to say.

My poetry is never going away.

www.ingramcontent.com/pod-product-compliance
Ingram Content Group UK Ltd.
Pitfield, Milton Keynes, MK11 3LW, UK
UKHW041822200726
13854UKWH00001BA/447